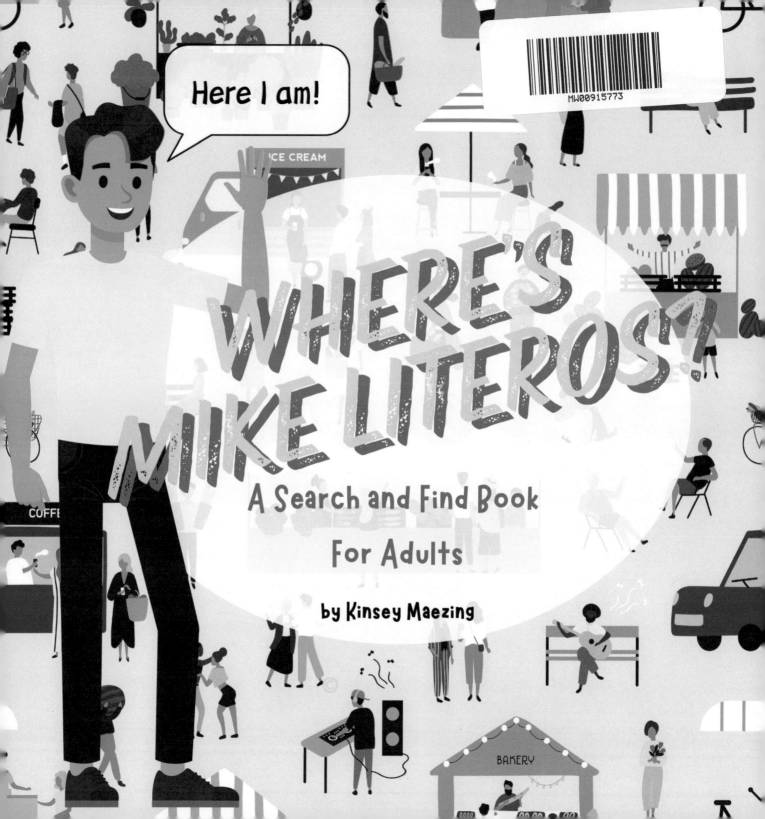

Mike Literos is hiding somewhere in each scene.
Do you have what it takes to find Mike Literos,
or is it too hard for you?

Mike Literos is enjoying some fun in the sun.

Mike Literos enjoys a good thrill ride.

Mike Literos enjoying the white stuff.

Mike Literos enjoying some good vibrations.

Mike Literos is enjoying the crowd.

Mike Literos is waiting for the train.

Mike Literos is out of this world!

Dedicated to all
those able to find
Mike Literos.

It shouldn't be that hard.
🫰

Find all of Kinsey Maezing's adult parody books on Amazon.

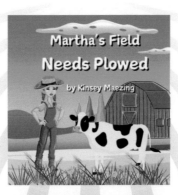

28061818R00017